SIMPLE MOTIVATIONAL GUIDE FOR CREATING WEALTH

Philemon I. Gora

authorHOUSE®

AuthorHouse™ UK Ltd.
500 Avebury Boulevard
Central Milton Keynes, MK9 2BE
www.authorhouse.co.uk
Phone: 08001974150

First published by AuthorHouse 01/22/2011

ISBN: 978-1-4567-7331-1 (sc)
ISBN: 978-1-4567-7332-8 (e)

Contents

INTRODUCTION

We live in the part of the world where many people believe that wealth is meant for a selected few or for the advanced countries alone. On the other hand, some people believe that one has to be lucky to be wealthy. But I have come to discover that is not true.

Everyone can create wealth suitable to him or her. As a matter of fact, wealth is not really in the amassment of money but actually a state of well being. A state where you are comfortable and peaceful about life.

From my experiences and practices which have given me some measure of well being I have brought you some principles that would motivate you to take step in creating the fortune you desire in life.

I have tried to be simple in this first book in my motivational series because being simple is better in getting greater results.

We live in a country (Nigeria) which is highly blessed with resources. This country has wealth at every corner you turn. But the sad thing is that not everyone is living in wealth. The reason been that not everyone has learnt the principles meant to create wealth. We are looking at wealth every now and then, but we can't see it nor handle it.

We must engage our mind therefore to create wealth from what we have. We have all the resources needed to make fortune out of life. But that alone is not enough. We must humble ourselves to learn the principles needed to turn our resources to a blessing.

You have in your hands a little book that will do great things in your life.

Join me as I bring you simple motivational guide in creating wealth.

Guide One

YOUR PURPOSE HOLDS YOUR WEALTH

Let me start this book by saying that your purpose holds your wealth. Your true wealth is within your true existence for living on this earth. You cannot separate wealth from purpose.

You see, you start creating wealth the very moment you discover why you are living or what you are living for. This is because purpose gives meaning to everything on earth. Without purpose therefore creating wealth will be a burden and a waste.

So to create wealth therefore there is every need to discover purpose. I must say that you are not a mistake, no matter how you come into the world. How and where you were conceived is not as importance as why you were conceived.

The world may not think much of you but you are somebody with a purpose and on a mission. The fact that you were born, means you are somebody special on assignment to this place called Earth. You are not here to escort others, neither were you created to be a spectator. No matter your present financial state you are somebody.

Whatever your background, you can be a voice and an influence in your own little corner. Your smallness can be turned into greatness. Remember, every great man was once a small man, every professor was once a students, every rich family was once a poor family, every celebrity was once uncelebrated.

One of the mysteries of life is that anybody can become anything. God is a specialist in turning nobody into somebody. Nobody was ever born second class. Nobody was born with a lesser brain.

I know of a woman who was born illegitimately. She was naturally unwanted and rejected by her mother. Her mother was so irritated with her that she put her inside a pit toilet but today she is a great woman in our society.

Purpose discovering questions

If purpose is a key to wealth, then it is necessary to discover purpose. To do this, I have brought some questions that would help you. I would want you to think deep before you answer them because the answers you give will lead you to a life driven by purpose and ultimately begin the creation of wealth for you.

Who do I want to become? What am I learning? What do I truly want out of life? How could I contribute to making this world a better place? What problems am I solving? What problems am I creating? What am I committed to? Who do I love? How will I help others? What am I excited about? What legacies do I want to leave behind? How and for what will people remember me?

What are my standards, value and beliefs? What must I do to reach my destiny? When and where do I start?

Be committed to your purpose

What you need in life is not sympathy, but courage to act on your conviction and dreams.

If you have a burning desire and dream to be somebody, you can. But to live without a dream means death in disguise. The world can never notice and stand up for a man who has no dream or purpose. See beyond your present condition and don't allow anybody put a limitation on you.

Don't ever feel guilty about dreaming big and thinking big.

That's one reason you have a mind. All achievers have similar drives. That is, to rise above the crowd. You have to think big and do extraordinary things.

One of the worst things you can do to your self is to devalue and demean your self due to circumstances or environment. Never count yourself out of the contest of life. Regardless of what people think or say about you, you can secure a good place in the race of life. Always remind yourself that you are somebody. You are a child of destiny, don't abort your greatness. All you need do is to be committed to your purpose.

I want you to know that within you is wealth. As you get committed to pursuing your purpose the more you realize that wealth is easy to create. I want you to give your purpose all it would required because as you fulfil it you get wealth in return.

Guide Two

KEY TO CREATING WEALTH

I want to bring one fundamental key to creating wealth. I believe without this key life itself will be miserable. No matter what you desire, ambition or dreams may be, its' success is anchored on this key.

The fundamental key to creating wealth is knowledge, and I mean wealth-creating-knowledge. It is popularly said that knowledge is power. Knowledge is not just power, but it is also creative and proficient for a fruitful living. The worth of life is limited to the knowledge at your disposal. Likewise, wealth is limited to the knowledge you operate with. What you know is the key to your relevance.

Knowledge gives you wings to rise above the crowd. What you know gives you an edge in creating wealth and fortune for yourself. Knowledge is a requisite to making good out of life.

In this country, if you must create wealth, then you must have at your disposal knowledge that would make it possible.

Knowledge enhances your abilities; it sharpens your skill, and upgrades your mind. Sound knowledge is an asset to wealth. It gives power, worth and value to everyone that has it and effectively puts to use.

Today knowledge has power, it control access to opportunity and advancement. Advancements in knowledge always pay the best interest. Knowledge helps you make a living, while wisdom helps you to make a living.

Those deficient in knowledge do not have guaranteed destiny. Only the knowledgeable can answer questions and provide solutions to the needs of the society and man. Nothing is more terrible than to see ignorance in action. The easiest way to keep people in darkness and prison is through ignorance, because ignorance incapacitates people. You see, poor or wrong decisions are all product of ignorance.

Knowledge is what gives you value in financial matters. It is the combination of all that we know and what we do with what we know that determine what we get out of life.

Knowledge makes life easier. To enjoy good life, you have to be a better person. To be a better person you have to live in the correct atmosphere of knowledge. If you are not getting the desire result of what you want, change what you know and operate with.

Many people especially the youth that I have interacted with do desire financial fortune. But the sad thing is that little percent of them have the knowledge required for creating wealth. It is good to have a dream, but without knowledge dream will remain imagery rather a reality. Just as you have a strong desire for wealth so equally you must have a strong craving for knowledge that would make your dream a reality.

It is vital to point out that lack of knowledge does not necessarily mean the head is empty. It could simply mean misinformation or wrong assumption. You know some people suffer in life more from what they know, or think they know, than what they don't know.

You must enrol in the school of improvements, and engage yourself in study. While others are sleeping, and develop, your skill. While others are just wishing, be a hunter of knowledge. What ever your business or profession things will get better when you know a little more.

Invest on good books

The mind is the most important tool and asset for progress and wealth creation in life. It is the best computer ever built by the Creator. However the performance of the mind is determined by what (information) you put into it and how developed it is through meditation.

I am an advocate of reading, but I believe material worth reading should enlighten, polish, update and upgrade the quality of our thinking to a level where we respond positively to the issues of life. Remember our decisions in life determine our destiny. And these decisions are the products of the information we feed our minds with.

Our walk to destiny therefore, begins with information. This information now determines the knowledge with which we build our lives. While wrong information is cancerous to life, good and positive information is a treasure and asset to making life count.

Investing in good books that contain the information that necessitate wealth creation is a must for a better life. No amount of money is too much to be paid for information that guarantees the realization of your dream. Go for books especially financial books in the bid to creating a fortune out of life. I would not just want you to buy the books, magazines, etc, but you must equally digest them in order to develop the knowledge required for bringing your wealth making dream a reality.

The quality of information you feed your mind with determines the quality of life you lead. What dominates our thinking will always become our reality. The companies you keep determine the way you think and act. One of such influential forces is the written word.

Great men and women have taken time to hide the best of their thought, ideas and visions in books. The reading of good books has been responsible for turning the lives of many around. It has made winners out of losers.

The truth is that any secret you are looking for is hidden in one book or the other. Someone rightly said, "Reading is the way out of ignorance, and the road of achievements."

Books are documented thoughts needed for better tomorrow. Books are hidden treasures. They are more or less the easiest means to interact with great and superiors minds which we may not be privileged to meet physically.

It is pertinent to understand that anytime you read a book, it makes you think life the author. That means the things we read or hear are some of the greatest influence of life.

You can run ahead your peers if you become a habitual reader and thinker. Reading is to the mind what exercise is to the body. A healthy mind cannot be easily caged. Nobody is too old or too young or too engage, or too poor to learn.

Don't forget one of the secret that makes men great is the books they read. Books expand and stretch our mind beyond our limitation. They cheer up, encourage, and open our mind to see possibilities. Books are good companions

It is impossible to read a good book and not make a fortune out of life.

Organize your knowledge for wealth creation

Knowledge will not attract wealth, unless it is organized, and intelligently directed through practical plans of action. Lack of understanding of this has been the source of confusion to many people who falsely believe that "Knowledge on its own is power". It is nothing of the sort! Knowledge is only potential power. It become proficient power only when and if it is organized into definite plans of action and directed to a definite end.

Knowledge has no profit unless it is tailored to a goal, and at this time the goal is creating wealth. I encourage you to have a plan that every knowledge you acquire will bring you closer to wealth that you so dream of.

Apply your knowledge

Wisdom is what we define as the accurate application of knowledge. You will not be financially wise until you apply the financial knowledge you have acquired. You see, knowledge will never profit you until you apply it. It is in the application of knowledge that wealth is created.

Over the years, I have come to discover that everybody, regardless of his or her vocation needs wisdom in order to live meaningful, progressive, victorious and productive life. This is because everything that works in life operates through the instrumentality of wisdom. This is why we are admonished scripturally to ask God for wisdom.

Wisdom is the tree of life and the vehicle that conveys us to our destiny. When applied it brings alongside glory and honour. Wisdom is the pathway to dignity and the master key to achievement.

Wisdom is the right application of knowledge. It is knowledge of the truth guided by understanding. Wisdom is knowing which way to go, what to do, how to do it and when to do it. It is doing things in the right way at the right time with the right people for the right reasons.

The ants are an amazing and wonderful creature. This tiny "insignificant" insect, which could be crushed to death by one tread of foot, teach us a lot about wisdom for productive living. They live tragically short lives, yet accomplish so much. Studying the ant we find foresight, diligence and hard work, the ants prove to us that wisdom includes been industrious, patient, persistent, perseverance, stamina, planning, organization, communal living and the power of teamwork and networking.

King Solomon counselled. "Go into the ant you slogan and be wise. They have neither king nor ruler but they gather their foot in the summer waiting for the winter".

If we must create wealth we should go for the required knowledge.

Guide Three

ENGAGING THE MIND FOR WEALTH CREATION

Life is measured by its duration but by donations. Some of the people who impacted the world positively did not really live long but they live long enough to make a difference.

Every productive and meaningful life is a product of good mind. I know of a company's statement that says "good thinking good product". The mind is the centre of all human activity. It is the seat of knowledge and wisdom. The mind is where reasoning, thinking, remembrance, decisions, imagination and analysis take place. It is the faculty of our intelligence and the seat of our will and emotions. The worst kind of disability is not therefore that of the body but the disability of the mind.

It is important therefore to note that wealth creation begins in the mind. Until it is in the mind, it cannot become a reality. The Scripture admonished us to always guide your hearts "with all diligence for out of it are the issues of life".

You must engage your mind to proffer wealth generating solutions. The mind must be dutifully used to produce wealth creating ideas. Until this is done, you may never live in wealth.

Your mind is your greatest asset in life. But you have to engage it in creative and productive thinking in order for it to bring you its dividends.

A good mind is what makes a good man. If a man can change the way he thinks, he will change the way he lives.

It is important to know that if you take good care of your mind, your mind will take good care of you. For according to Shakespeare, its thinking that makes a man.

Use your mind productively

You are what you think about. Until you use your mind to think wealth, it will be difficult to create it.

The human being is a very complex and sophisticated creature. What makes him unique above all other creatures is his mental capacity. The human mind has been referred to as "the most complex living mechanism in the world".

The mind is a place where thought are incubated. It is also a place that makes the body rich. A man's destiny can never be separated from his thoughts. The size of your thinking determines how far you go in life. People who can not think are not qualified to make headway in life. Until you put on your thinking cap, a very little worth, value, respect and dignity is accorded to you. You can never divorce the accomplishment of a man from his thoughts.

A man who cannot think is not only an embarrassment to his destiny, but a liability to his generation. There can be no productive and meaningful life without a sound mind.

A man is a product of his thought. So, the mind must be use to think creatively and productively in order to create wealth. It is therefore important to know that to waste the mind is to destroy life.

Until you win in the mind you can't win any where else. All great thinkers are ordinary people that used their minds greatly. All great dreamers and achiever were great thinkers. Everything you see around you is a product of some one's thought e.g. cars, books, computers, cloths, electricity, and road network, just everything.

Every progress or backwardness ever faced by humanity is a result of thinking. Our modern world is the creation and crowning achievement of the thought of others. You don't have to go to school to make it in life, but you must use your mind to succeed.

Life becomes excellent only when we think positive and healthy thought. Negative thinking destroys potentials, paralyses visions and immobilizes purposes.

Remember, our modern world is built by positively minded people, that is, people who take the right actions in the right direction.

Good thinkers are problem solvers; Good thinkers are big thinkers and up thinkers. Wherever you find a good thinker, you have just found a good man, a good citizen and a potentially good leader.

Progress is never achieved by doing the wrong thing. John Locke said "the actions of men are the best interpreters of their thoughts". To think well, we must think up.

Learn to renew your mind by fixing it on what is good and right. Think about things that are pure and lovely and dwell on the good things of life. Think about the good things in others. Think about all you can praise your creator for and be glad about.

Productive thinking is what makes a better world, start now and don't delay. It will create a fortune for you in shortest time.

Guide your mind

Many are limited not because they don't have ability but because they are careless about what is being fed into their minds. They don't care enough to eliminate those things that tend to destroy and limit them from reaching their destiny. They allow pollutant in their mind to poison, impede, and distort their focus, which eventually impairs their vision

The good news about your mind is that you have absolute control of it. You can determine what goes into it. It is like the computer language that says "garbage in, garbage out (GIGO)". The mind is basically nourished by words (things we hear and read) and those things we see, touch and smell. We must dare to change our thought life, by reading good book and associating with the right people, and going to the right places.

Your thought determines your beliefs, your beliefs control your attitudes, and your attitudes expose your decision, which ultimately determines your destiny. The most important asset that will cause you to have a place and relevance here on planet earth is your mind, therefore protect it. Remember to always polish upgrade, update and renew your mind.

A good mind is what makes a good man. If a man can change the way he thinks, he will change the way he lives. A great philosopher reminds us that, "it is not enough to have a good mind, the main things is to use it well."

Guide Four

THE POWER OF FAITH IN WEALTH CREATION

As an illustration, consider the purpose for which you are reading this book. The object is, naturally, to acquire the ability to transmute your intangible thoughts into wealth. However it must be accepted that you can never become what you do not believe. So in this study, we would examine some steps to putting the power of faith to work in creating the fortune we desire.

1. *Believe you can*

The first step to creating wealth is to believe you can create one that is peculiar to you. Believe in your abilities. Believe in your idea and God's grace to realize it.

The foundation to create wealth is to believe that you can. Once the belief is within you, there would be the courage to dare it. Many people dream of making wealth but never believe they can make it. Due to this, they fail even before they try. Peradventure they tried and failed, they get discouraged and quit.

If you must have good fortune in life, then believe you have the capacity to make one. Do not think or believe that you cannot make it. You are so endowed with abilities and resources to create wealth.

Do not allow the present economy and your challenge to discourage you. Do not doubt your ability to make wealth. Have the faith within you.

There are millions of people who believe themselves are "doomed" to poverty and failure, because of some strange force over which they believe they have no control. They are the creators of their own "misfortunes" because of this negative belief, which is picked up by the subconscious mind.

2. *Guide your mind*

You must guide your mind against negative thoughts and influence. Every thought that goes contrary to the possibility of you creating wealth should be discarded. King Solomon said, "keep your mind with all diligence, for out of it are the issues of life". One reason you are to guide your mind is because your mind is the seat of faith.

Be positive in your thought. Be optimistic in your approach.

You can create wealth from where you are if only you believe.

Do not fill your mind with fear, doubt and unbelief in your ability. Let 'I-can-create-wealth' mentality flood your heart and enthusiastically go ahead making your future real.

3. *Go for information*

Faith is of the mind and it is developed through information. The information you feed your mind with determines what you will become. If you feed your mind with the information of doubt, fear, failure, defeat and impossibilities, definitely doubt will occupy your mind. And this will result to inferiority complex which paralysis your ability to create wealth.

But on the contrary, if you feed your mind with positive thoughts, ideas, possibilities, courage, hope etc. then faith will be built for wealth creation.

4. *Relate with wealth minded people*

I have come to appreciate the fact that your associates greatly define your future. Those that associate with the rich will be rich. This is because they will learn the secret and encourage each other to implement them. As a result, they all grow to be rich.

To build faith for wealth, you must not forget to associate with those that want to be wealthy. You cannot associate with the poverty expecting individuals and become rich. Remember someone said, show me your friends and I will tell you who you are.

Make friends with those that have believe in creating wealth.

Guide Five

CREATING WEALTH THROUGH YOUR GIFT

In creating wealth, I must make it emphatic that your inbuilt and acquired gift, skill or ability plays major role. Without your skill, gift, talent, potential or ability, you may never be able to create wealth. As a matter of fact wealth comes at the moment you begin to utilize your gift.

You see, every creature has inbuilt gift, skill, talent or ability that is purposefully given in order to create a living. For instance, within a mango seed, is the ability to become a plant, produce mango fruit, juice etc. But until these abilities are used, the mango would not bring out the wealth hidden in it as the fruit, herbs, juice etc.

Likewise, within you are gifts that are originally built in you to enable you create wealth. You have the required resources to create the level of wealth that you so desire.

In his book *"Your Gift Is Your Asset"*, Wisdom Emamuzo Peter gave some interesting definition of gift. Few of his definitions are: 'Gift is a natural ability that dwells in you, that is your inborn ability needed to fulfil any assignment. Gift is a given ability to cause change as it relates to power, which means gift is a dynamic ability to cause desired changes in the course of fulfilling a purposes.'

Wealth is created at the moment you discover and begin to exploit your gift. Many persons are poor today not because the economy of our country is very hard, but because they have failed to use the gift that is lying dormant in them.

Your true wealth is potentially your gift.

Discover your gift

For instance, imagine how wealthy some of the musicians are! Michael Jackson became wealthy through his gift of singing and dancing. I believe no other job would have given him such wealth in life. You see, all that wealth he had were within him but never came to be until he discovered and began to use his gift of singing and dancing.

Likewise you! Wealth is within your reach if only you would discover your gift and begin to use it. Many persons created their wealth through the gift of writing, oration, leadership, negotiation and communication, etc. You will never become rich beyond your gift or ability. Your wealth is truly hidden in your abilities.

I have found out that we are paid for the use of our abilities. The nature of ability exploit determines the level of wages you are given. This is the reason why those that utilizes more of their mental ability are more and well paid.

My gift of marketing, negotiation and communication is creating wealth for me. You purchased this book because

I put my writing gift to use. Interestingly, you have added to my financial fortune.

You see, your prosperity, wealth and riches are within your reach if you could discover and use your hidden abilities.

Develop your gift

Discovered gift does not necessarily bring wealth. You have to develop it to the level it could attract wealth to you. The more you develop your gift the more wealth it could potentially create for you.

For instance, the gift of communication has lot of money to bring your way. But that is not enough. You need to develop your communicating gift. Everybody is talking, many are writing but not all are making fortune from communication. The reason is not everyone has taken time to develop that gift.

The more you develop your gift the more it will be sought for. And the more it is sought for, the more wealth it would create for you.

Discover and develop your gift, then you are on your way to creating wealth.

Utilize your gift

You begin to create wealth at the moment you start using your gift. So, do not just discover or develop your gift, but utilize it. Until you utilize your gift, it has no power to create wealth for you in the real sense.

In utilizing your gift, you must begin to seek out opportunities favourable to your gift. Look out for avenues that would bring you fortune as you put your gift to work.

It is a popular saying that "Rome was not built in a day". However, it all started in a day. You must begin to use your gift today if you must build wealth for tomorrow.

If you are gifted in communication, seek opportunities that you would utilize it and bring you wealth. One aspect of communication that is bringing wealth to young people in this country, Nigeria, is Comedy. These comedians are making good fortune from making people laugh. Your true wealth is lying within your gift.

Manage your gift

Management is a core virtue to wealth creation. You will never be wealthier than your managerial ability. Until you are able to manage what you have, you will not be able to effectively use it bring your true desired result.

Now that you have discovered; developed and are already to use your gift, you must take a great step to managing your gift. Don't sell off what you have. Make it your own and manage it until it brings you real wealth. This is because wealth is not always overnight. It comes in stages. And the stages are determined by your managerial ability.

In summary, I want you to follow the DDUM formula for wealth creation.

D: Discover your gift to lay the foundation for wealth

D: Develop your gift for real wealth

U: Utilize your gift to bring you the wealth.

M: Manage your gift to maintain the wealth you have created.

Guide Six

UNIVERSAL RESOURCES FOR WEALTH CREATION

Under this Guide, I want to help you with what I called the universal resources for wealth creation. Many people think or believe that money is the only resource for wealth creation. This is not very true. Money may not bring wealth. This is because money is one tool to creating wealth. However, in this Guide I am not considering money as universal resource. This is because so many persons became wealthy not necessarily through money but by good working knowledge and exploitation of these other resources.

It should be accepted that these resources are universal and at the disposition of everyone. But the sad thing is that many persons have not giving good attention to them. Let's consider them:

TIME

The first universal resource for wealth creation is time. Life itself is a product of time. Without time, nothing exists and nothing is meaningful.

Wealth comes at the accurate and productive use of time. Wealth is created at the moment time is prudently used for with purpose. Everything answers to time. This is one of the reason we have a popular adage that says "time is money".

Time is a gift given to every living creature under the sun. Every person living on the earth has equal and but irreversible time allotted to us. No one has more time than the other.

But you see, while others are using their time to create wealth, others are using their time to destroy their wealth. While others are investing time, others are whiling or wasting away time.

You see, during my National Youth Service days, while I was creating wealth with my time, other fellow Youth Service Corp members thought it not necessary with the hope that as soon as they leave the service one big job would land on their laps. You must learn to have a good seizure of time. For there in lie your wealth.

On a regular basis, you have to stand back and take stock of yourself and what you're doing. You have to stop the clock and do some serious thinking about whom you are and where you are going. You have to evaluate your activities in the light of what is really important to you. You must master your time rather than becoming a slave to the constant flow of events. You have to organize your life to achieve balance, harmony, and inner peace.

Time is your most precious resource. It is the most valuable thing you have. It is irreplaceable and irrecoverable. All work requires time. And time is absolutely essential for the creation of wealth and fortune.

I want to help you understand some usefulness of time and why you should make it duty to use it effectively.

Take time to evaluate your present financial state

You need time to evaluate your present state before you take step. You see, the reason why some people won't leave the position they are, it is because they have not really taken time to evaluate their position and what the future may be as a result of where they are.

You will never make progress until you evaluate your present state. You have to evaluate your financial position and what your future financial state would be based on your present situation.

Take time to set priorities

There are three key questions that you can ask yourself continually to keep your personal life balance. The first question is "What is really important to me? Whenever you find yourself with too much to do list and with too little time, stop and ask yourself "What is it that is really important for me to do in this situation?" then make sure that what you are doing is the answer to that question.

The second question is, "What are my highest valued activities?" in my personal life, this means, "What are the things that I do that give me the greatest pleasure and satisfaction?" "Of all the things that I could be doing, what are the things that I could do to add the greatest value to my life and finance?"

And the final question to ask over and over is, "What is the valuable use of my time right now?" Since you can only do one thing at a time, you must constantly organize your life so that you can do, the most important thing, at every moment. Personal time management enables you to choose what to do first and what not to do at all.

Setting priorities enable you to organize every aspect of your life so that you can get the greatest joy, happiness, and satisfaction out of everything you do.

Take time to gather information

To create wealth, you must have relevant information. And information that would help you to create a fortune. Gathering information requires time, this is because, good information is not found on the surface but deep in the heart of the earth.

For instance, you want your financial growth to be on the progress, and then you would need to gather relevant information on financial management so as to meet your financial desire. And not until you have gotten the information needed to achieve your goal, you may only be day-dreaming but never would get what you want. It has been said that knowledge is power because through it wealth is built. But you need time to gather the information that will bring out the knowledge you need to have your needs met.

Take time to meditate

One good thing to start life with is goal setting. However, goal set does not necessarily mean goal achieved. There are some things to do in order to achieve the set goal.

In creating wealth, one thing you must do with the information you have gathered is meditation. Meditation simply means pondering over an issue with the intention to proffering solution or working out steps to achieving a goal.

One hard thing to do is to meditate. This is why not many people get involved in meditation. Those that think create wealth and fortune. Check out all the inventors, manufacturers, administrators, etc. they are all thinkers.

I learned of Bill Gate who once asked his mother "Mum, don't you think?" His wealth is not a product of education or inheritance but a product of meditation.

Now to think or meditate, you actually need time. This is because meditation is time consuming and investing. As you meditate, you are activating the brain cells for maximum productivity and creativity. The result of this mental exercise would be a fortune created. Don't use your time for things that won't bring you fortune. Take time to engage your senses, it will produce wealth for you.

Take time to implement

Lastly, I want to encourage you to take time to implement the ideas or solutions you got through meditation. This is because knowledge is only powerful when implemented. Information or knowledge you do not work with, would never bring you your desired result.

Many people are still in the place they were financially because they have not put to practice what they have learned on building finance. If you have taken time to read this book to this point, then you should do yourself good by implementing whatever knowledge or idea you have gotten which would help you realize the wealth dream that you have.

IDEA

The next universal resource for creating wealth which I want to share with you is idea.

Idea is wealth!

No one has ever become financially great without an idea. Idea has remained the singular propelling force behind the creation of wealth and fortune all over the world.

Telephone was an idea. Automobile was an idea. Computer, air planes, clothes, etc. are all ideas that came through some persons. And their humble attitude in implementing the ideas has never left the world the same.

Idea is not meant for some selected few but to everyone from all race, culture and geographical location. However, it must be accepted that ideas though available to all, not everyone will actually have ideas that would bring wealth.

One sound idea is all you need to commence the creation of wealth. And there is nothing too much to be paid for sound idea. To create wealth you must become 'idea hunter'.

Success is nothing but the realization of ideas. Until you have got good idea, you are yet to begin the race to true wealth. Idea is a universal resource because any person can have one by engaging the mind.

COURAGE

One of the most common causes of failure is the habit of quitting when one is overtaken by temporary defeat. The road to success is not always free from distractions, failures, temporal defeats, challenges.

But universally, everyone that has create wealth has used their challenges as stepping stones to where they were going. The ability to forge ahead in the midst of challenge is what I referred to as courage.

Wealth does not come by wishing or daydreaming. It does not come on the rosy path. Interestingly it comes through challenges and failures. However, study has shown that those that are wealthy did that by studying their challenges and proffering solutions to turning the challenge to fortune.

Courage is not meant for a few people but for all. Howbeit, only those that take advantage of it will benefit from it.

I encourage you today not to concentrate on the deteriorating economy, your present challenge or the disappointment you have gotten in the past. It is time to be courageous and create the wealth you have so dream.

As you take courage in pursuing your dream, I want you to know that success comes to those who are success conscious, while failure comes to those who defeat conscious. No matter where you are, you can create the future you so desire. Be courageous.

PEOPLE
Human resource has remain one of the greatest assets we are blessed with. No matter your dreams, visions, ideas, and purpose, one sure resource you would need to attain it is human being.

People are every where. But that does not mean they will be of help to you in the realization of your dream for creating wealth. You need to develop good and respectful relationship with people in order for them to assist you gets what you want from life.

It is a popular saying that no man is an island of his own. This means, we all need one another to succeed. Many people do say that they don't have any person to help them. This is not very true. There are people every where. What we need is to develop healthy relationship with them.

Remember, that human being is a universal resource for wealth creation. Many people became wealthy today through some one else. Tap into this resource today.

ENVIRONMENT

To create wealth, you must learn to tap the potentials of your environment. Within your environment are opportunities that when exploit will bring you good fortune.

Wealth is always around us if only we could see into our surrounding. A young graduate saw so many refuses littering the city he was and got an idea. The idea was to clear the rubbish from people's compound for a certain amount. He went to the government and they approved a pit for him to dump the refuse. He began the job, and today, he has employees working in his company. Now he is wealthy.

You see, everyone saw a dirty environment but this fellow saw wealth in the dirt. How you see your environment determines what you get from it. I may not know the exact place you are staying in Nigeria or rest of the world, but I am sure there is wealth lying below the earth for you.

OPPORTUNITY

It may interest you to know that wealth is a product of your ability and opportunity. You cannot separate the two. If you must create wealth in these present days, you must be very keen to discover what your abilities are and the opportunities available to you.

The inabilities of some person to discover and understand the opportunities available to them have kept them in poverty. Nothing makes one great like opportunities exploited. The fact is; opportunity is the base for the creation of wealth. This is because no matter your ideas, dreams and abilities, if there are no opportunities that could bring them to reality; they would only remain a mirage.

Opportunity is everywhere and so, it is available to everyone. But it will only profit and bring fortune to those who could discover it and exploit it. One interesting thing about opportunity is that it mostly comes as challenge, problem, difficult situation and unpleasant condition. But belly in that situation is a well of wealth.

Guide Seven

TWO PRACTICAL STEPS TO CREATING WEALTH

Having learned much in this simple book, I would want to bring you some practical steps needed to creating wealth.

SET WEALTH CREATING GOAL

To create wealth, you must begin by setting wealth creating goals. Until you set goals for wealth making, you will not achieve any. This is why some people work hard to make money yet the money is not within their reach. The reason is that they do not have goal they want to achieve.

You must set financial achievable goals. Goal is what you want. At this time your goal should be wealth. My journey into fortune actually began from goal setting.

For instance you have to set goal that every one thousand naira (N1, 000.00) you have will work for you to bring again more than half of it. With this goal, you would want to put you one thousand naira (N1, 000.00) in the right area that would make it multiply itself.

Have goal for your time and resources.

It is needful to say that, your goal must be measurable and achievable. Do not set goal for setting sake. For instance you can have a yearly goal of adding 20% increase to your present income. And that this 20% would come from your investment.

Personal time management begins with you. It begins with your thinking about what is really important to you in life. It only makes sense if you organize your time and resource around the specific thing that you want to accomplish. You need to set goals in three major areas of your life. First, you need family and personal goals. These are the reasons you get up in the morning, work hard and upgrade your skills, why you worry about money and sometime feel frustrated by the demands on your time.

What are your personal and family goals, both tangible and intangible? A tangible family goal could be a bigger house, a better car, a lager television set, a vacation or any thing that cost money. An intangible goal could be to build a higher quality relationship with your spouse and children, to spend more time with your family going for work or reading good books. Achieving this family and personal goals are the real essence of time management, and its major purpose.

The second areas of goals are your business and career goal. These are the "how" goals, the means by which you achieve your personal goals which are your "why" goals. How can you achieve the level of income that will enable you achieve your family goals? How can you develop the skills and abilities to stay ahead of the curve in your career? Business and career goal are absolutely essential, especially when balanced with family and personal goals.

The third type of goals is your personal development goals. Remember, you can't achieve much on the outside than what you have achieved on the inside. Your outer life will be a reflection of your inner life. If you wish to achieve worthwhile things in your personal and career life, you must become a worthwhile person in your own self-development. Your must build yourself if you want to build your life. Perhaps the greatest secret of success is that you can become anything you really want to through determination. But in order to do it, you must work on yourself and never stop.

Once you have a list of your personal and family goal, your business and career goals, and your self-development goals, you can then organize the list by priority.

DRAW OUT WEALTH CREATING PLAN

Goal is what you want to achieve. But that you have a goal does not really mean you would achieve it. There is more to setting goal. The next step to take is to plan how to achieve your goal.

Goals are achieved not because they are only set but because they are planned for. You must have a working plan to achieving your goal. Why setting goal, you talk about what to achieve, while by drawing a plan, you talk about how to achieve the set goal.

You can not create wealth outside plan. A plan is a step by step approach to creating a fortune for your self.

Guide Eight

UNDERSTANDING MONEY MOVEMENT

As we learn to create wealth in a country like Nigeria and all parts of the third world countries, it is important we understand how money moves in wealth creation. Many people are poor in this country not because money do not get to their hands or because they do not make money, but because they lack the knowledge of money movement.

Money movement in this context is how money either moves into our hands or out of our hands.

Every body gets money

Nigeria is one of the wealthiest countries where many people get money for free. Many of us get money for free which we do not work for. Someone can just freely give you a thousand naira (N1000.00) ($6.60 or £4) for just visiting him or her. Not because of a job done, but just because he want to. I have discovered that not only do we get free money from others, Nigeria is also one the freest countries in the whole world where everyone could easily make money. Just anything could bring money to you in Nigeria.

So, you see, money is circulating in this country but the problem is; we do not have the knowledge of money movement. And due to this, there is no amount of money that comes to us stays or grows; it just goes back to where it came from.

Many people work hard for the money, yet, within few minutes or days, they are financially broke. Where is the money they have worked for? It has all gone to where it came from.

You see, friend, many of us are poor because we do not understand what money is and how it ought to flow. Permit me to help us understand the logic money have played over our intelligence for long a time. However, to everyone like you who is seriously minded in having good financial stand must endeavour to read other financial materials. This will go a long way increasing your understanding in financial matters.

Investment versus Expenses zone

Money moves towards two directions. Money moves either towards investment or expenditure. What I mean is that, the money you receive either through work or free gift, will always move from your hands to these areas: that is, you either invest it or spend it. However, the direction of its movement is determined by you.

When you let money move from your hand into the investment zone, it create more money for you in the future. And the more you do this, the more money you create, thus, creating financial wealth.

On the other hand, when you let money move from your hands to the expenses zone, it brings no money in return. And the more you spend, the more you get financially broke; thus, becoming poor.

Please in this context, I am considering money spent to be money used that will not bring any money to you in return. You get nothing back from it. Many of us in this country and other third world countries are very good at spending – that is putting money in areas or things that will bring no financial return. Permit me to say in this other way that, we are go waster of money.

But, when you invest money, it means you spent it on things that will bring more money to you in the nearby future. This is how you create financial wealth. In a simpler way, investing money brings you more money, while spending your money takes more money from you or you have wasted the money that would have brought you more money.

The difference between the rich and the poor is their understanding of money movement. While the rich get richer by putting money into what would bring more money in the future, the poor puts money to areas that would always take the little they have from them. The rich multiplies their money by investing it, while the poor reduces their money to almost zero by wasting the one they have. We are not poor because we don't have money. No! We are poor because we put our money on areas that make us bankrupt

If you must create financial wealth, you must learn to invest money on what will bring money to you. Don't spend money on what will take even the little you have from you without getting anything back. With this understanding, I have diversified my money making avenues. Now I get money from my speaking engagements, writing, lectures, farm, enterprise, forex trading, etc. The more money I invest in these areas, the more money I get in return. I even get more than money. For instance, I have gained a wider recognition from my writing and speaking engagements.

Simple Addition and Multiplication Logic

When you spend on investment zone, your money increase in two ways: addition and multiplication.

You money increases in a slow pace when you put your money on the investment zone of addition. But it increases rapidly when you put it on the investment zone of multiplication.

For instance, shares are good and secure investment that brings more money to you in the future. But this is investment zone of addition because the returns comes slowly and most often in a longer pace.

But when you invest probably on real estate that is investment zone of multiplication. You can purchase a property in a good area and within two years the profit margin would be so amazing. This is multiplication investment zone. This is because you may get more than twice of what you invested.

The bottom line is that the direction you move your money into determine either you are creating wealth or destroying your future wealth.

Move your money and income to the investment zone today.

Guide Nine

FINANCIAL INTELLIGENCE

Intelligence solves problems and produce money. Money without financial intelligence is money soon gone. Most people fail to realize that in life, it is not how much money you make, its how much money you keep. And you keep and multiply money through financial intelligence.

The big problem of the Africans, I think, is not lack of resources. Our big problem is lack of intelligence. We are poor not because we don't have the resources to make everyone wealthy, but majority of us lack financial intelligence.

If you want to be rich you must begin to develop your financial intelligence. Most people struggle financially because they do not know the differences between an asset and liability.

Wealth comes through asset, while it goes out without return through liability. If you want to become wealthy in life, then you must choose to invest on asset. The opposite is very true to remain poor in life: that is wasting money on liabilities. You see, the rich people acquire assets while the poor and middle classes acquire liabilities, which unfortunately, they think they are assets.

Difference between Asset and Liability

Asset	Liability
An asset is something that puts money into your pocket.	Liability is something that takes money out of your pocket.
An asset creates wealth.	Liability destroys wealth.
An asset establishes inflow of cash.	Liability establishes the outflow of cash.
An asset creates more assets.	Liability creates more liability.

This is really all you need to know. If you want to be rich, simply invest your resources on buying assets. But if you want to be poor or in the middle class, then spend your life buying liabilities. Let me give you a brief illustration here:

This book you are reading is one of my assets. The money started coming when I began teaching the principles. Now the money is multiplied because the principles are in a book form. Presently, the book is one of my sources of income. It flows in cash for me. It is not a liability at all. I chose to put my money into it because I knew what the returns would be on a regular basis and from around the world.

On the other hand, I have seen young people taking pride in owning two to three mobile phones. One sad thing is that, they are not working and so, to get more air time is a problem. Some go to the extent of begging just to recharge their phones. What stops them from owning just one and invest the money of the other one.

You see, if what you have do not contribute to you, it is already a liability no matter how good it may appear. Liability steals away our future wealth in the present. While asset creates, secures and promotes our future wealth even from today. You can not create wealth by going for liabilities. Wealth is within the sphere of asset.

Questions that makes you wealth conscious

I want you to think on these questions deeply in order to become wealth conscious. You may not need to send me your answer, let the answer prompt you into action.

Do I have an asset?

What do I have that can be regarded as an asset to me?

Do I have a land, building, business of my own?

What I have presently is it taking money, peace, joy and comfort from me or is it bringing me problems?

CREATING WEALTH THROUGH BLOG

Do you have a blog? Your blog can turn into a money maker and generate enough money for you. Blogging full time is no longer a wishful thought nor is it a privilege for the rich and famous to cash in on their fame.

A blog is mainly used to spread articles, adverts, and create interactions between you and your readers. With the help of blogging, you bring your products, ideas, services before the world without much stress. It is cheap and faster in reaching a wide range of audience. Through blogging, you can make good fortune.

Starting a blog is not hard; just ask your self questions like these. However, you must be computer literate and be a good user of the internet facilities.

What are you passionate about?

What keeps you talking for at least an hour?

What do your friends and family comes to you for advice?

Once you identified your niche its time to get started. You can start blogging on free platform like www.blogger.com or www.wordpress.com

As you publish your posts, you should create what is called Key Words. Keywords are search term that you type into a search engine such as Goggle that helps in searching a desired result. Now with your key words, whenever someone is looking for anything that contains your key words, your site and related article would display on the result from the search engine.

Finally, making money require you to put in real effort to build a blog that benefits the web community. A good blog attracts lots of loyal readers and these translate to more cash. Remember the only reason people fail is that they either do not try or they quit.

HOW TO MAKE MONEY FROM YOUR BLOG

This is the most important parts of these reports. If you want to make money from your blog then you should be able to work. In fact I suggest investing at least two hours a day for the next 30 days non- stopping.

After setting up your blog like www.cashflow4love. blogspot.com, the next thing will be to start using it to make money. You do this by reaching people through your blog in relating to them the product you have to offer by writing articles.

In fact if after today for next 30days you should be able to summit at least 1 to 2 articles everyday.

Follow this process

Go to www.ezinearticles.com and open an account. It is free. The beautiful thing about article marketing is that as long as people are reading it you will keep making money.

LEARN TO MARKET YOUR INFORMATION OR IDEAS

Information marketing is one business you must get involve. I make lot money from this business as well as from other source.

However, you should be wise in marketing your information because it is one slippery asset at your disposal. Don't give your wealth creating information away without any return.

I do earnestly advise that you visit www.cashflow4love. blogspot.com to learn the step by step on how to build a five figure information business in Nigeria. Ensure you read that reports and put the principle into work

Understanding Cost per Action (C. P. A.) MARKETING

You see there are companies online that are ready and willing to pay you from $7 to $15 dollars (about N1050 to N2250 Nigeria currency) for the visitors you send to them who take a simple action like filling a form or downloading a free soft ware. Some pay higher than the given estimate while others pay lesser. The bottom line is that you get paid for introducing people to them.

For a start, I would want you to visit www.zangocash. com, www.affiliiatesseeking.com/pay-per-lead.html and follow the given instructions.

Guide Ten

INVESTING IN THE SHARES AND STOCK MARKET

I want to encourage you to invest in shares and stock market. It helps to create wealth silently for you while you sleep. Take advantage of any advertisement on share offer and purchase some unit. With the help of a stock broker, you would be able to make good dividends from your shares.

If you are not familiar with this kind of investment, let me enlighten you briefly. A share is the unit value of a company which the public can buy. When you buy any unit of shares; you become a "share-holder." How much of the company you own is determine by the unit of shares you are able to buy. Due to this, when the company declares its' profit at the end of its' financial year the profits would be shared to all shareholders based on the unit of shares they have. This is what is referred to as "dividend" of a share.

However, to reward shareholders, the company may also give "free shares" to its shareholders. It may be one free share to four existing shares. Because the free shares is valued as the other shares, that increases your stock. That free share is called a "bonus"

There are two ways to buy into a company and begin to make money. The first is through an initial public offer (IPO) where the company offers its share to the public, mostly, at a little discount.

The second is by buying shares on the flow of the stock exchange, this known to be the secondary market.

The stock exchange is like an open market where shares are trade daily. You will however do trading through its' authorize traders called "stockbrokers".

Trading on the floor of stock exchange require some skill. You need to understand the market indicators. Again you should know when to buy and when to sell. The general rule is to buy when the price is low and sell when the price is high. The difference will be your profit.

Caution!

Just it is important to invest in the stock market, you must be very careful on which company you are to buy shares. Don't rush in and buy shares in any company that placed an advert. You have to study the company and understand their profit margins. Study to know what kind of business they are doing. You must know whether what they do brings returns faster or not.

Just as you take the right steps in creating wealth, I wish you the best of financial rest.

For speaking and seminar engagement, you can contract Philemon I. Gora by email: cashflow4love@ yahoo.com or call: +2347037085199, +234808281719